Foreword

The recipes in this book have been popular with our guests at Pleasant Hill. I hope you will find them useful to you in your own home, and that they will serve as a pleasant reminder of the Trustees' House, where "we make you kindly welcome."

We have one special advantage in cooking at Pleasant Hill. Garden vegetables are always best; if you're lucky enough to have your garden just outside your window—as we do at the Trustees' House—you can have the season's freshest within reach. But if you don't, select the best you can find. A patch of mint or (even better) a small bed of herbs can enliven your meals—and furnish a fresh-scented and attractive "herb bouquet" for the center of your kitchen table.

Always use the best possible quality of canned and frozen goods and gelatin desserts, too; it makes a difference in appearance as well as in taste, and food is best when it pleases the eye as well as the appetite. Be sure to serve your hot foods hot and your cold foods cold; a lukewarm temperature dulls the best dish.

I've found certain kitchen tools essential: wooden spoons and wire wisks for stirring; a variety of jello molds for salads, especially ring molds; a pastry cutter for crusts; and *heavy* irons (skillets, muffin pans, cornstick pans), the older, the better. (Incidentally, if you have a hearth, you can "burn off" your old iron skillets in the open flame of a winter fire, then wash and re-season them. This makes a cooking surface no modern skillet can rival.)

The organization of this cookbook follows the menus of the Trustees' House, giving specialties of Morning Daily Fare, Midday Daily Fare, Evening Daily Fare, Sunday and Holiday Daily Fare, and Special Daily Fare. The *Index* at the end is for your convenience in looking up particular items. The following abbreviations are used:

T = Tablespoon
C = Cup
tsp = teaspoon

oz = ounce
pt = pint
lb = pound
gal = gallon

I wish to thank my cousin, Robert B. Jewell, for introducing me to Shakertown, itself; Mildred E. Elliott, who shared the venture of the Summer Kitchen with me; my niece, Betty W. Morris, and my daughters, Anna K. Reed and Evalina K. Settle, who put this book together; James L. Cogar and all the people who have helped, especially my dear kitchen staff at the Trustees' House; and Earl D. Wallace, who first said, "Elizabeth, can't you get a cookbook together for us?"

Elizabeth C. Kremer

History

Pleasant Hill was a village of nearly 500 members of the United Society of Believers in Christ's Second Appearing—men and women who separated themselves from "the world" and abandoned "the carnal life." These disciples of Mother Ann Lee observed celibacy and common ownership of goods; and they "shook out" their sins in a religious ceremony for refreshment of spirit from which they got the name *Shaker*.

Shakers were careful workmen, both practical and inventive. They experimented with scientific farming, designed agricultural tools, and developed new breeds of sheep, hogs and cattle. They marketed brooms, preserves, garden seeds and herbs known throughout the country for quality. The venture—which began in 1805 with three Mercer County farmers and ended in 1910 with the passing of the property to private hands—was a fine flowering of idealism, dedication and integrity.

Today the small village of twenty-four buildings is owned by Shakertown at Pleasant Hill, a non-profit organization which seeks to maintain the simplicity and dignity of the 19th century settlement. Located high above the palisades of the Kentucky River twenty-two miles southwest of Lexington and seven miles northeast of Harrodsburg, this village offers the public a glimpse of the Shaker community and a pleasant vacation from the rush of the world.

Exhibition houses and workshops furnished with original Shaker pieces are open to the public. Lodgings with private baths are available in restored buildings—where air-conditioned rooms are furnished with reproductions of original Shaker pieces and hand-woven curtains and rugs. Meals are served in four dining rooms in the Trustees' House—or Trustees' Office as it was originally called—where in past days gentle Shaker Sisters graciously offered bountiful but simple meals to guests.

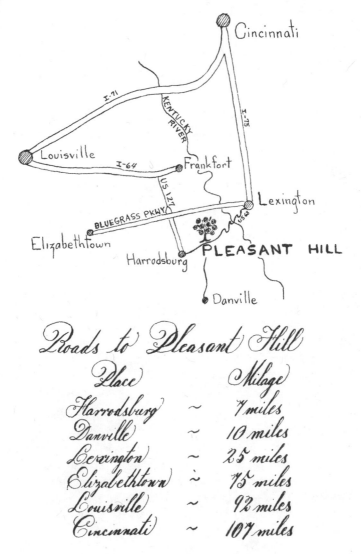

Roads to Pleasant Hill

Place		Milage
Harrodsburg	~	7 miles
Danville	~	10 miles
Lexington	~	25 miles
Elizabethtown	~	75 miles
Louisville	~	92 miles
Cincinnati	~	107 miles

Food at Pleasant Hill
A Tradition of Excellence and Courtesy

From its earliest days the Shaker Community at Pleasant Hill observed a tradition of good food and service. The journals of 1840 and 1850 note details of the fall in-gathering: "Gathered apples for jelly and apple butter"; "Went after hickory nuts, 22 sisters and 2 brothers began to pull corn"; "Commenced cutting and drying pumpkins." The observance of Thanksgiving was marked yearly with "all business suspended."

Hungry travelers came to Pleasant Hill for food and shelter; they were welcomed. Some wanderers stayed as temporary converts, accepting the Shaker way of life (and Shaker hospitality) for a brief season. "Winter Shakers," as they were wryly called, converted at the onset of cold weather, then changed their minds in the Spring; some came year after year and continued to find a welcome.

And Pleasant Hill's Shakers always met the needs of the world they had renounced. The civil war found them feeding each side with graciousness:

> August 12, 1862. A company of 100 United States Cavalry in transit encamped in our pastures east of the East Barn. We gave them supper and breakfast in the Office yard and fed the horses at the camp; also gave them lunch when they left at noon being ordered back to Harrodsburg. . . .
>
> October 12, 1862. Colonel Gano of General Morgan's command came and ordered breakfast for 200 troops, which was produced with alacrity, and they came in from the Lexington road where they had encamped. . . . During this time the Sisters were cooking and baking with all the means at their command to keep a supply till about 400 had eaten.
>
> *(Journal, Pleasant Hill)*

Shaker Elder Henry Blinn, of the Canterbury Community in New Hampshire, noted in his journal the hospitality of Pleasant Hill after a visit in 1873: "The good sisters brought Br. Micajah and the writer an excellent dinner. Our table was spread in one of the best rooms in the dwelling house." The same excellence was characteristic a decade later, as John M. Cromwell (father of the author of this cookbook) recalled in his column in the *Cynthiana Democrat:*

> Here I recalled a most bountiful meal taken with the Shakers. In 1886 I happened to be one of a party of about a dozen wheel men. After climbing the long hill we were in a receptive mood for a square meal, and the hour being high noon we decided to try our luck with the Shakers. Never shall I forget the meal we sat down to on that occasion. Like "Oliver Twist" we asked for more, but unlike him we were not denied. That's been a long time ago, but I still remember a demure little Shaker lass that waited at our table. She was a beauty and of course the boys tried to "start something": and not a chance. Have often wondered if some fortunate swain didn't come along and persuade her to renounce the celibate life. Quien sabe?
>
> ("Cromwell's Comments," *Cynthiana Democrat,*
> May 26, 1930)

Similar recollections of Pleasant Hill were cited by Dr. George M. McClure, the Danville educator, in an interview with Gerald Griffin of the *Courier-Journal:*

> Like the other Shakers at Pleasant Hill, Sister Jane Hutton, who presided over the public dining room, went about her business quietly, speaking but little although courteously answering her visitors' questions with a smiling "Yea" or "Nay."
>
> Dr. McClure, nationally recognized as a benefactor of the deaf, connects Sister Jane with his courtship in 1884 when a dinner at Shakertown was considered a social highlight by Danville folks. And a meal at Pleasant Hill he considered a "Lucullan feast" to use his own words, and Dr. McClure isn't a man to exaggerate.
>
> Young people of Danville often organized parties to drive in fringe-topped surreys — well-chaperoned, of course — all the way to Shakertown for dinner. It is 13 miles. They didn't need to make reservations. The dinner guests merely drove up to the house which then housed the dining room, hitched their horses and announced their presence to Sister Jane. She always expressed pleasure in welcoming them. She enjoyed visits from "the world."
>
> —GERALD GRIFFIN, *The Courier-Journal*
> Sunday Supplement, April 1962

When the Shaker property went to private hands, the tradition of excellence and courtesy remained; "the world" continued to come. During the 1920's and 30's Mrs. Nannie Jewell Embry had a tearoom marked for its delicious food and popular throughout Central Kentucky.

Shakertown at Pleasant Hill, Inc., organized in 1961, made plans for the continuation of Shaker hospitality, including a concern for food and service. In 1967 Elizabeth C. Kremer and Mildred Elliott presided over a Summer Kitchen in the Old Stone Shop. The next year the present restaurant in the Trustees' House was opened under the direction of Mrs. Kremer. Here you may enjoy "Daily Fare," breakfast, lunch and dinner, in one of three dining rooms or on the porch overlooking Shaker lands. Waitresses, dressed in Shaker garb, seek to recapture the courtesy and simplicity of the days when the Shaker sisters served their guests on white dishes at well-scrubbed wooden tables, supervised by the Kitchen Deaconess who reminded them to give "their hands to work and their hearts to God."

View of Shakertown

Shakertown at Pleasant Hill
Trustees' House
Morning Daily Fare

Breakfast

Choice of Fruit or Juice
Buttered Toast   or   Hot Biscuits
with Jam, Jelly, or Maple Syrup
or
Shaker Sweet Bread

Breakfast

Choice of Fruit or Juice
Indian Griddle Cakes with Syrup

Breakfast

Choice of Fruit or Juice
Two Eggs with Bacon or Sausage
Buttered Toast   or   Hot Biscuits
Shaker Sweet Bread

BREAKFAST CANTALOUPE

Cut cantaloupe in six or eight wedges and clean out seeds. With a sharp knife loosen tender meat from the rind on each wedge. Do not remove the meat from the rind; slice it in ½ inch chunks. Offset the slices, leaving the end pieces in place. Serve the cantaloupe with a thin slice of lime and a sprig of mint.

BISCUITS

1 C flour   9 T sweet milk
½ tsp salt   3 T shortening
1½ tsp baking powder

Sift dry ingredients. Cut shortening into flour. Make a well in the center of the flour and put milk into the well. Stir until the dough cleans the bowl—not over ½ minute. Knead it ½ minute. Pat it out on a floured surface to about ½ inch or to desired thickness. Cut with 2 inch biscuit cutter. Bake at 425° for 10 minutes or until golden brown. The cooked biscuits (cooled) can be stored in a tin or frozen and used later.

BLACKBERRY PRESERVES

fresh, well-washed blackberries
sugar

Mash the blackberries with a potato masher. Measure the pulp and add one pt of sugar to each pt of pulp. Bring the mixture to a full bubble and cook 30 minutes.

Be sure to *skim* the mixture while it is in the pot, so that the paraffin will seal properly. The best skimmer is a wooden spoon.

Ladle the preserves into sterilized jars. Melt paraffin carefully, removing all bubbles with a sterilized spoon. Pour it until it is about ¼ inch thick on top of each jar of preserves. Let it stand and harden.

FRIED APPLES

2 qt small and tart apples
⅓ box light brown sugar

1 good pinch of cinnamon
⅓ stick butter or margarine

Cut unpeeled apples in six wedges from core to stem; remove the seeds. Place the apples in a skillet; sprinkle them with sugar and cinnamon, and dot with butter.

Cover the skillet with a lid or foil; place it on a cold stove. Set at low heat and cook until tender, stirring only occasionally. Remove the lid and cook 3 to 5 minutes longer.

INDIAN GRIDDLE CAKES

½ tsp salt
½ tsp soda
3 tsp sugar
½ tsp baking powder
2 T oil

1 egg
½ C flour
1 C buttermilk
1 C plus 2 T corn meal
sweet milk

Mix, beating well, all ingredients except the sweet milk. When the mixture is smooth, add enough sweet milk to make the consistency of the batter thin. Heat a griddle covered with melted shortening until very hot. Dip about ¼ C batter to each cake. Fry until bubbly on the top and light brown on the bottom. Flip and cook until done.

GLAZED BREAKFAST FRUIT

4 pears   ¼ box brown sugar
4 peaches   ¼ stick butter
6 apricots

Place fruit in sections in shallow buttered baking dish. Sprinkle with brown sugar and dot with butter. Bake at 450° for 15-20 minutes.

(If you have good country sorghum molasses, it may be substituted for the brown sugar.)

SCRAMBLED EGGS

2 T strained bacon grease   6 eggs
½ C milk (Cream is even better.)

Beat eggs and milk together for about 30 seconds. Melt and heat bacon grease in skillet or heavy pan until it begins to sizzle. Pour egg mixture into skillet and cook over low heat, scraping back and forth with a spatula. Do not overcook; eggs should be moist and fluffy.

PUMPKIN MUFFINS

¾ C brown sugar   1 C cooked mashed pumpkin
¼ C molasses   1 tsp soda
½ C soft butter   ¼ tsp salt
1 beaten egg   1¾ C flour
¼ C pecans

Cook, drain and mash the pumpkin; put it through a strainer.
Cream sugar, molasses and butter; add egg and pumpkin and blend well. Mix the flour with soda and salt; beat this mixture into the pumpkin batter. Fold in pecans.
Fill well-greased muffin pans about half-full with batter; bake at 375° for 20 minutes. Makes 1¼ dozen.

(These muffins may be frozen and kept until company comes for breakfast.)

SQUASH MUFFINS

¾ C brown sugar
¼ C molasses
½ C soft butter
1 beaten egg
¼ C pecans

1 C cooked mashed squash
1 tsp soda
¼ tsp salt
1¾ C flour

Cook, drain and mash squash to the consistency of mashed potatoes.

Cream sugar, molasses and butter; add egg and squash and blend well. Mix flour with soda and salt; beat this mixture into the squash batter. Fold in pecans.

Fill well-greased muffin pans about half full with batter; bake at 375° for 20 minutes. Makes 1¼ dozen.

(This is an excellent recipe for people who don't like squash. The squash gives the necessary batter, but the flavor comes from the molasses.)

NUTBREAD

2 C flour
¾ C sugar
1 T baking powder
1 C unsweetened applesauce
½ tsp nutmeg

1 tsp salt
¼ C oil
1 beaten egg
1 C chopped nuts
½ tsp soda

Mix the sifted dry ingredients and the nuts together. Combine the egg, applesauce and oil; add these to the dry ingredients and stir until blended. Pour the mixture into a 5 x 9 greased pan and bake at 350° for 50 minutes.

SWEET BREAD

½ C milk   ½ C warm water
½ C sugar   2 packages or cake yeast
1½ tsp salt   2 beaten eggs
¼ C butter   4½ C flour

Add the sugar and butter to scalded hot milk; cool until luke-warm. Warm the water and place it in a large, warm bowl. Crumble in the yeast and stir until it is dissolved. Stir in the lukewarm milk mixture, beaten eggs and one half of the flour. Beat until smooth; then stir in the remainder of the flour until the dough is stiff; work it down for 4 or 5 minutes. Place the dough, buttered on top, in a bowl; let it double in size.

Roll or press it out, pushing out the bubbles as you go. Make the dough as square as possible. Spread it heavily with melted butter, and sprinkle it with a mixture of brown sugar and butter; then sprinkle raisins on top.

Roll it up like a long jelly roll. Slice it into 1 inch slices; place them on a greased sheet and let them rise another hour. Bake them at 350° for about 20 to 25 minutes. Spread them with glaze (see below) while they are still hot.

Glaze for Sweet Bread: Mix powdered sugar and water. Make the glaze thin and refrigerate it; this will give it a good spreading consistency.

(Rolls may be baked in advance and frozen. Add the glaze after reheating the rolls at 350°.)

Notes

Shakertown at Pleasant Hill
Trustees' House
Mid~Day Daily Fare

Small Tenderloin Steak on Toast
Shaker Dish of the Day
Country Ham Sandwich
Filet of Sole
Pleasant Hill Salad Plate

Vegetables and Salad will be passed

Village Hot Breads

Desserts

Shaker Lemon Pie   Special Dessert
Chess Pie   Seasonal Tart
Sherbert or Ice Cream and Cookies

Coffee   Milk   Tea   Buttermilk

Shaker Dress

CREAM DE VOLAILLE

3 C chicken ground with
  ½ C mushrooms
1 C thick white sauce
  T butter

3 beaten eggs
2 tsp salt
⅓ tsp red pepper
a little chopped parsley

Mix white sauce with chicken and mushrooms. Add butter and eggs; beat the mixture very hard. Add seasoning and a little chopped parsley. Pour mixture into a greased mold. Cover mold tightly with foil; place it in a shallow pan filled with about ½ inch water. Put both in oven and steam at 400° for 1½ hours. Serve with Mushroom Cream Sauce. (See p. 59.)

CHICKEN HASH

1¾ C chicken broth
¼ C chopped onion
⅛ tsp black pepper
1/16 tsp red pepper
¾ tsp salt
⅛ tsp seasoning salt

2 T butter
3½ C chicken
½ C flour shaken
  with ¼ C cold water
  to make paste

Heat the broth and add the seasonings; taste for seasoning *before* adding the thickening. Shake flour and water together for thickening; add this gradually to the broth. Add the chicken pieces, then the butter.

(This may be served with Indian Griddle Cakes, p. 4.)

11

COUNTRY MEAT LOAF

1½ lbs ground beef
½ C finely chopped onion
¼ tsp pepper
1½ tsp salt
1 egg

¾ C oatmeal
2 T celery, diced
2 T green pepper, diced
1 C tomato juice

Beat egg slightly. Add beef, onion, salt, pepper, celery, green pepper. Toss with a fork until blended: for a light loaf avoid packing the ingredients during mixing. Lightly stir in tomato juice, then oatmeal. Shape into loaf and put in aluminum foil on rack in pan; be sure to spread foil so that fat runs away from loaf. Bake at 350° for 1½ hours.

CHEESE CASSEROLE

4 slices of bread
2 slices of cheese
salt and pepper
butter

2 C milk
3 well beaten eggs
dash of tobasco

Butter bread and make cheese sandwiches. Butter baking dish and place sandwiches in the bottom, cutting them to fit your casserole.

Mix eggs and milk together, beating well; add seasonings; pour mixture over sandwiches. Let stand at least 3 hours in refrigerator. Sprinkle a little grated cheese on top. Bake at 325° for 1 hour.

This may be made the day before and baked when ready to use. It may be served with strips of crisp bacon on top.

CHICKEN KEENE

Meat from 1 cooked hen
salt to taste
⅛ tsp pepper
⅓ C butter
⅓ C flour
sherry to taste

1 C chicken broth
1½ C milk or cream
½ lb mushrooms
1 pimiento in strips
1 green pepper in strips

Melt butter in double boiler; stir in flour slowly. Gradually add chicken broth, then milk or cream. Cook until thickened, stirring constantly. Season. Add cubed chicken, mushrooms, pimiento, green pepper, and sherry. Serve in tart shell and sprinkle with paprika before serving.

STUFFED PEPPERS

4 medium-sized green peppers
2 T butter or drippings
1 medium onion, chopped
½ lb ground chuck
1 C canned tomatoes

1 tsp salt
pinch of pepper
1 C coarse bread crumbs
⅓ C buttered cracker or
    bread crumbs for top

Brown onion and ground chuck until slightly cooked; add tomatoes, cut into pieces. Add salt and pepper, then bread crumbs. Clean out peppers, leaving shells; stuff them with meat mixture. Sprinkle top with grated cheese and buttered crumbs. Bake at 350° 24 to 30 minutes.

PLEASANT HILL SALAD PLATE WITH COUNTRY HAM BISCUITS AND CHICKEN SALAD

3 packages lemon gelatin dessert   Melon balls in summer
2 oranges, sliced and drained   3 C hot water
1½ grapefruits, sliced and drained   1 C cold water
Berries or fruit in season   1 small can fruit cocktail

Dissolve gelatin dessert in hot water; then stir in cold water. Put small amount of gelatin dessert in mold and place fruit of the season decoratively around mold; place in refrigerator and let set. Add rest of fruit gently; do not let mold become warm; add remaining gelatin dessert and return to refrigerator. Unmold salad and serve section on outer leaves of lettuce with chicken salad and country ham biscuits. Put a dab of mayonnaise on top of salad, Decorate with parsley.

COUNTRY HAM BISCUITS

Mix ground country ham with enough country dressing to produce a smooth consistency. Spread mixture on cooked biscuits. Heat at 425° about 5 minutes or until very hot.

CHICKEN SALAD

1 lb cooked chicken   ¼ tsp seasoning salt
¾ C country dressing   ¼ tsp salt
¼ C mayoñaise   ¼ tsp red pepper
¼ C chopped pecans   ¾ C chopped celery

Cut chicken in cubes with scissors, mix with celery, fold in country dressing, then mayonnaise and pecans. Top with mayonnaise when serving.

STEWED TOMATO QUARTERS

½ C melted butter   1 full T sugar
1 T chopped onion   ¼ tsp salt
1 large can tomato quarters   ⅛ tsp black pepper
   (or fresh tomatoes)   1½ T chopped green pepper

Melt butter in heavy skillet. Add onion and cook lightly, but do not brown. Add remaining ingredients and cook gently and quickly.

BAKED APPLESAUCE

Mix cinnamon and sugar in applesauce to taste. Heat in pan on top of stove. Then place hot applesauce in shallow baking dish. Top with marshmallow. Bake in oven at 350° until marshmallows are golden brown. Serve immediately.

(Either large or miniature marshmallows may be used. The miniature ones look better, but if your family likes marshmallows, use the large ones.)

BAKED TINY PINEAPPLE

1 large can pineapple rings   ½ C sugar
   (tiny Malayan are best)   3 T flour
1½ C pineapple juice (from can)   ¼ C butter

Place pineapple rings in shallow baking dish. Bring juice and butter to a boil in a sauce pan. Mix flour and sugar together and add to boiling juice very slowly. Cook until slightly thick. Pour this over pineapple rings and bake 30 minutes at 350°.

BAKED ZUCCHINI AND TOMATOES

2 medium zucchini	salt and pepper
2 medium tomatoes	butter
1 medium mild onion	1 C crushed butter crackers

Wash zucchini; do not peel unless the skin is hard. Peel the tomatoes and onions. Slice all vegetables into very thin crosswise slices. In a greased baking dish make alternate layers of zucchini, tomatoes, and onions, sprinkling each layer with a little salt and pepper and dotting with butter. Cover the top with crushed cracker crumbs. Bake at 350° until vegetables are tender.

HOMINY GRITS CASSEROLE

1 C hominy grits	1 C grated sharp cheese
4 C water	2 eggs
1 tsp salt	1½ C milk (approx.)
½ C butter	corn flakes

Cook grits in boiling salted water until slightly thick; add the cheese, butter, and salt. Cool a little. Put eggs in measuring cup and add enough milk for 1½ C; then beat. Fold egg mixture into grits. Put in 325° oven for 15 minutes. Stir and sprinkle with corn flakes and cook until firm.

GLAZED CARROTS

1 qt canned carrots	2 T butter
(small Belgium carrots are best)	½ C brown sugar

Drain the carrots. Place them in a baking dish, sprinkle with sugar, and dot with butter. Bake at 450° for about 20 minutes.

If fresh carrots are used, pare, boil until tender, then proceed as above.

STUFFED ZUCCHINI

6 medium zucchini
3 C butter crackers
½ C grated Parmesan cheese
1 small onion, minced
3 T parsley, minced

⅛ tsp pepper
1 tsp salt   .
2 eggs, beaten
2 T butter

Wash zucchini and cut off ends, but do not peel. Cook in boiling salted water for 5 minutes or until tender. Halve lengthwise. Remove pulp with spoon. Combine pulp, crackers, cheese, onion, parsley, salt, pepper, and eggs. Fill zucchini shells with mixture and dot with butter. Sprinkle with additional cheese and bake at 350° for 30 minutes.

OCTOBER SALAD

1 package apple gelatin dessert
1 C boiling water
½ C cold water

½ C chopped dates
1 C diced red apples, not pared
1 C diced pears

Dissolve gelatin dessert in hot water. Add ½ C cold water. Chill slightly. Add other ingredients and pour into wet mold. Serve with ginger salad dressing.

GARDEN GREEN SALAD

2 envelopes unflavored gelatin
2½ C cold water
1 T finely chopped onion
½ C tarragon vinegar
½ C sugar
½ C grated carrots
½ C celery

1 tsp salt
½ C chopped pimiento
1 C whole canned green beans
¾ C sliced canned mushroom
   (or cooked fresh
   mushrooms)

Sprinkle gelatin over ½C cold water in saucepan; stir in onion. Place pan over low heat; stir constantly until gelatin is dissolved, about 3 minutes. Stir in remaining 2 C water, vinegar, sugar, and salt. Chill until slightly thickened; fold in remaining ingredients. Pour into wet mold and chill until firm.

SHAKERTOWN COLE SLAW

1 qt shredded cabbage	½ C commercial slaw dressing
¼ C shredded carrot	¼ C country dressing
¼ C chopped onion	¼ C mayonnaise
¼ C chopped celery	½ to ¾ tsp salt

Mix all together. If too dry, add more country dressing. (Cabbage, when old, is sometimes very dry.)

ICE BOX ROLLS

1 cake yeast	1 tsp salt
1 egg	7 C flour
½ C sugar	1 C plus 1 T melted shortening
2 cups water, slightly cooler than lukewarm	

Crumble yeast in crock (or bowl); add water, then egg slightly beaten. Add sugar, salt, and about ½ of flour. Then add melted shortening and rest of flour. Place in warm spot (*e.g.* on back of stove) and let rise about double (approximately 2 hours). Press down, cover, and put in refrigerator overnight. Roll out on floured board and cut with small biscuit cutter. Butter slightly. Fold over. Put in pans (preferably tubular pans) and let rise in warm place until light (puffy). Cook at 450° until light brown (approximately 10-15 minutes).

(Rolls should be worked as little as possible and placed in a warm spot to rise quickly. This recipe may be used for cloverleaf rolls or dinner rolls and baked in a cake pan. Ours are baked in a tubular pan.)

SHAKER LEMON PIE

2 large lemons	2 C sugar
4 eggs, well beaten	

Slice lemons as thin as paper, rind and all. Combine with sugar; mix well. Let stand 2 hours, or preferably overnight, blending occasionally. Add beaten eggs to lemon mixture; mix well. Turn into nine inch pie shell, arranging lemon slices evenly. Cover with top crust. Cut several slits near center. Bake at 450° for 15 minutes. Reduce heat to 375° and bake for about 20 minutes or until silver knife inserted near edge of pie comes out clean. Cool before serving.

—From recipe in *The Shaker Cook Book*
by Caroline B. Piercy.

BREAD PUDDING

about 4 C stale bread
¼ tsp salt
3 C warm milk
½ C sugar

3 eggs
1 tsp vanilla
½ tsp nutmeg

Crumble stale bread. Soak for 20 minutes in milk and salt. Combine eggs, sugar, vanilla, and nutmeg; beat very well. Pour mixture over the bread; stir lightly. Steam tightly covered with foil in pan set in hot water for about 45 minutes at 350°. Cover with meringue and bake at 300° for 15 minutes. Serve with Brown Sugar Sauce. (See below.)

BROWN SUGAR SAUCE FOR BREAD PUDDING

½ lb brown sugar
¼ C flour
1 C boiling water

¼ C butter
½ tsp vanilla

Mix sugar and flour well. Add boiling water. Cook mixture until thick. Remove from fire and add butter and vanilla.

EGG KISSES

4 egg whites
½ tsp vanilla

2 C sugar

Beat the whites of the eggs with the sugar until the mixture is very stiff. Flavor with vanilla and drop from teaspoon in small rounds on a baking sheet that has been lined with brown paper. Cook 20 minutes at 250°.

(Serve with fresh strawberries or fruit in season. Or serve with orange ice. Top with unsweetened whipped cream.)

APPLE COBBLER

7 full C sliced apples
¾ C sugar
¼ tsp nutmeg
⅛ tsp salt

1 T lemon juice
½ tsp grated lemon rind
¼ tsp cinnamon
2 T butter

Place apples in pan. Sprinkle them with all ingredients and dot with butter. Top with pie crust; prick crust or cut slits in it. Bake at 350° for 1 hour.

PECAN PIE

3 slightly beaten eggs
1 C light corn syrup
1 C brown sugar
1 C pecans

⅓ C butter
⅛ tsp salt
1 tsp vanilla

Mix together and fold in slightly beaten eggs. Fold in pecans. Pour into unbaked pie shell. Bake at 350° for 1 hour.

OATMEAL CAKE

1 C quick cooking oats
1¼ C boiling water
½ C butter
2 eggs
1 C brown sugar
1 C white sugar

1½ C flour
1 tsp baking powder
½ tsp soda
½ tsp salt
1 tsp vanilla
1 tsp cinnamon

Pour boiling water over oats and let stand a few minutes. Combine butter, vanilla, eggs, and both sugars; add oatmeal mixture. Sift together remaining dry ingredients; add to mixture. Bake in lightly buttered long baking pan at 350° for 20 to 30 minutes.

While cake is still hot, pour topping (see below) over top. Run it under the broiler, long enough to slightly brown. Serve with unsweetened whipped cream.

TOPPING FOR OATMEAL CAKE

1 C brown sugar
½ C canned milk

4 tsp butter
1 C coconut

Mix all together and pour over cooked oatmeal cake.

PINEAPPLE UPSIDE DOWN CAKE

2¼ C flour
3 tsp baking powder
1 tsp salt
1½ C sugar

½ C shortening
⅞ C milk
2 eggs
1 tsp vanilla

Sift flour, baking powder, and salt. Cream shortening and sugar. Add eggs, slightly beaten. Mix well. Add flour and milk alternately. Stir in vanilla last.

2½ C crushed pineapple
½ C butter

2 C brown sugar (packed)

Melt the butter in heavy pan or skillet. Press brown sugar firmly into this. Place crushed pineapple evenly on sugar. (Slices or cubes may be used.)

Pour cake mixture in large skillet on top of pineapple. Bake at 325° for 30 to 40 minutes. Cool 5 minutes and turn out on platter.

CHOCOLATE DROP COOKIES

½ tsp baking soda
½ tsp salt
1 C plus 2 T flour
½ C butter
1 package chocolate drops
1 egg

6 T granulated sugar
6 T brown sugar, packed
½ tsp vanilla
¼ tsp water
½ C chopped pecans

Cream sugars and butter. Beat in egg, water and vanilla until smooth. Sift soda, salt and flour together; add to creamed mixture. Blend well. Add pecans and chocolate drops. Drop small dabs from a spoon onto greased cookie sheet. Bake at 375° for 6 to 8 minutes.

CHERRY COBBLER

1 qt cherries
1 C sugar
¼ C flour

¾ tsp lemon juice
¼ C butter

Drain cherries and reserve liquid. Add to liquid the sugar, flour, and lemon juice; mix well. Place cherries in pan and pour mixture over them. Dot with butter. Top with crust and bake at 350° for 45 minutes.

SHAWNEE RUN JAM CAKE

2 C light brown sugar, sifted	1 C jam, with seeds
2 C buttermilk	¾ C chopped nuts
1 C raisins	3 eggs, separated
3½ C flour, sifted	1 tsp cinnamon
2 tsp soda	1 tsp ground cloves
1 T cocoa	1 C butter

Cream butter and add brown sugar. Add beaten egg yolks. Beat well. Fold in jam. Roll nuts and raisins in ¼ C flour. Add cocoa and spices to remaining flour and sift again. Dissolve soda in buttermilk and add alternately with flour mixture, beginning and ending with flour. Add raisins and nuts. Fold in stiffly-beaten egg whites. Butter a 9 inch tube pan (or two loaf pans); line with brown paper or waxed paper. Turn batter into pans and bake at 250° until cake leaves side of pan. Turn out of pan and frost with Simple Caramel Frosting. (See below.)

(Ovens vary; some cooks bake this cake as high as 325°. I prefer a lower temperature.)

SIMPLE CARAMEL FROSTING
For Shawnee Run Jam Cake

¾ C butter	3 C powdered sugar
1½ C brown sugar	1 tsp vanilla
¼ C plus 2 T milk	

Melt butter and add brown sugar. Add milk and bring to a boil. Take off stove and let cool. Add powdered sugar and vanilla. Beat until creamy and smooth.

CHOCOLATE FUDGE PIE

2½ C brown sugar, well packed	½ C butter
3 eggs	½ C cream
½ square melted unsweetened chocolate	4 small squares german chocolate

Cream the butter and sugar well. Add eggs and beat all together. Mix in cream. Melt chocolates together and add to mixture. Pour into unbaked pastry shell and bake at 350° for 30 minutes; then reduce temperature to 225° for 50 minutes. Cool before serving. This can be served with whipped cream or with vanilla ice cream.

OATMEAL COOKIES

¾ C shortening
1 C brown sugar
½ C granulated sugar
1 egg
¼ C water

1 tsp vanilla
1 C sifted flour
1 tsp salt
½ tsp soda
3 C oatmeal

Cream shortening and sugars. Blend in egg, water and vanilla; mix well. Sift together flour, soda and salt. Add to shortening mixture and mix well. Stir in oatmeal. Drop by teaspoonful onto a greased cookie sheet. Bake at 350° for 12 to 15 minutes. Makes 5 dozen.

(If your family likes raisins, ¾ C may be added to the batter.)

OSGOOD PECAN PIE

1 C sugar
½ C butter
½ tsp cinnamon
½ tsp nutmeg

1 tsp vinegar
½ C pecan meats, broken
½ C raisins
2 eggs

Cream butter and sugar. Add cinnamon, nutmeg, vinegar, nut meats and raisins. Add well-beaten eggs. Pour in uncooked pie shell and bake 50 to 60 minutes at 350°.

Recipe furnished by DEEP SOUTH PECANS, Greenville, Alabama.

PEANUT BUTTERSCOTCH COOKIES

½ C plus 1 T butter
1 tsp vanilla
½ C brown sugar, firmly packed
½ C granulated sugar
½ C peanut butter
1 pk butterscotch morsels

1 egg
½ tsp salt
½ tsp soda
1 C flour
¼ C chopped nuts

Cream butter and peanut butter well. Add sugars and mix well. Beat in egg and vanilla til smooth. Sift dry ingredients together and gradually add to mixture. Stir in morsels and nuts. Drop by teaspoonful onto greased cookie sheet. Press lightly with sugared fork. Bake at 350° for 10 minutes.

Notes

Shakertown at Pleasant Hill
Trustees' House
Evening Daily Fare

Today Soup   Tomato Juice
Fruit of the Season   Fruit Juice

Egg in Aspic on Anchovy Toast

Pleasant Hill Chicken
Sirloin Steak
Country Ham
Filet of Sole
Shaker Dish of the Day

Vegetables and Salad will be passed

Village Hot Breads

Shaker Lemon Pie   Special Dessert
Chess Pie   Seasonal Tart

Ice Cream and Cookies

Coffee   Milk   Tea   Buttermilk

A Shaker Range

COUNTRY CHICKEN SOUP

1 carrot
¾ C celery
1 sweet green pepper
1 onion
¾ C cooked chicken, cubed
1 apple, peeled and sliced
    ¼ inch thick
4 T butter
⅓ C flour

about 1 tsp curry powder
2 whole cloves
1 sprig parsley
1 C canned or fresh tomatoes
4 C chicken broth (may be
    made from chicken bouillon
    cubes)
salt to taste
2½ to 3 C milk

Chop carrot, celery, green pepper and onion; fry lightly in butter, stirring often. Add chicken and all ingredients, except milk. Simmer with cover on for fifty minutes. Add milk; bring to boil. Serves 6.

VEGETABLE SOUP

2 lbs soup meat with 1 bone
4 qts water
1 T salt
1 onion, chopped
3 carrots, sliced
2 stalks celery, sliced
3½ C canned or fresh tomatoes

2 C okra
2 C butter beans
½ tsp sugar
¼ tsp ground cloves
1 tsp pepper
1 C barley

Simmer meat and bone in water with salt for 3 hours. Remove meat; dice it, and set it aside. Mash tomatoes and add to broth. Add vegetables and seasonings; cook 1 hour. Add barley and cook until barley is done. Add meat; season with salt and pepper to taste.

(Vegetable soup is always better the second day.)

POPCORN SOUP

2½ C fresh corn	½ medium onion
1 C milk	1½ tsp salt
3 T butter	dash of pepper
3 T flour	popcorn
2½ C milk	½ C half and half

Cook corn in milk until tender. Melt butter and saute onion until soft. Stir in flour, salt and pepper. Stir in additional milk, half and half, and add cooked corn. Sprinkle top of soup with popcorn before serving.

EGG IN ASPIC ON ANCHOVY TOAST

1 tsp gelatin	3 hard boiled eggs, halved
½ C water	crosswise
1½ tsp lemon juice	round toast
anchovy paste	1½ C hot beef consomme
	(canned)

Soften gelatin by sprinkling in ½ C cold water. Pour hot consomme over this and mix. Add lemon juice. Cool slightly and pour small amount (about ½ inch) into individual molds. (Small molds, about 1½ inch deep are preferable.) Place ½ hard boiled egg, cut side up, into this and chill until consomme is firm. Then fill molds with cooled consomme mixture and chill until firm. Turn out on crisp round toast spread with anchovy paste. Top with dressing made of mayonaise thinned slightly with milk and seasoned with lemon juice and tobasco sauce. Makes 6 servings.

(This is on the soft side and can be made more firm by adding additional gelatin. At the Trustees' House we prefer as little gelatin as possible, but the aspic must be served immediately.)

CHICKEN CASSEROLE

2 C diced cooked chicken	½ C mayonnaise
½ C pimientos	½ C milk
½ C celery	2 eggs
½ C onion	1 can mushrooms
½ C green pepper	1 can undiluted mushroom soup

Saute chopped celery, onions and green pepper. Mix with chicken pimientos, mushrooms and mayonnaise. Line baking dish with buttered bread squares. Spread ½ mixture over bread. Add another layer of buttered bread, then another layer of mixture. Beat eggs, add milk, and pour over all. Spread mushroom soup over top. Sprinkle with grated cheese and bake 45 minutes at 325°.

VEAL CUTLETS

Bread veal cutlets in cracked meal. Fry in small amount of hot shortening until tender and golden brown; turn only once.

Serve with mushroom sauce. (See below.)

MUSHROOM SAUCE FOR VEAL CUTLETS

¼ C butter	about ¼ C sherry (to taste)
1½ C drained mushrooms	¼ C flour
(stems and pieces)	¼ C water

Saute mushrooms slowly. Add flour slowly. Then add the juice of the mushrooms, water and sherry.

(This sauce is excellent served with broiled chicken livers.)

CHICKEN LIVERS ON TOAST WITH MUSHROOM SAUCE

Saute chicken livers in butter; do not overcook. Season with salt and coarse black pepper. Serve on toasted homemade bread. Top with mushroom sauce. (See above.)

CHICKEN CROQUETTES

4 C cooked chicken	½ C chopped celery
1 C mushrooms	½ tsp salt
2 C dry bread crumbs	dash lemon juice
1½ C chicken broth	⅛ tsp red pepper
1 tsp chopped onion	1 T chopped parsley
½ C melted butter	1 tsp chopped onion

Soak bread crumbs in broth; grind chicken and mushrooms. Mix all ingredients together. Let cool. Shape into croquettes (about 2 oz to each) and chill.

Dip into bread crumbs, then into beaten egg mixed with 2 T water or milk, then into bread crumbs again. (This is the secret of good croquettes.) Fry in deep fat. Serve with Mushroom Cream Sauce. (See p. 59.)

PORK TENDERLOINS AND CREAM GRAVY

Saute pork tenderloin in shortening and remove from pan. Keep warm. Use equal amounts of drippings to equal amounts of flour (about 2 T drippings and 2 T flour to 2 C milk). Heat drippings and sprinkle in the flour. Stir with wire wisk constantly and quickly and simmer until very smooth and bubbly. Remove pan from heat and stir in 2 C milk, again stirring quickly with wire wisk to prevent lumps. Return to heat; cook and stir until smooth. Season with salt and pepper.

KENTUCKY COUNTRY HAM

1 country ham	1 C vinegar
½ C whole cloves	1½ gal. water
1 C brown sugar	

Scrub ham. Soak in water overnight. Sprinkle some cloves in the bottom of roaster and some on top of ham. Add about one inch of water. Put remaining ingredients around ham. Set oven temperature at 375°; cook for 1 hour. Then turn temperature back to 275°; cook 20 minutes per pound. Remove from roaster; bone if desired. Trim if necessary.

Mix: 1 C brown sugar	1 T ground cloves
1 C corn meal	1 tsp cinnamon

Sprinkle ham with sugar, meal, cloves, and cinnamon. Brown in oven at 375°.

(Country ham is sugar cured, smoked, and hung—in the old days in smoke houses—and aged. An 18 month old ham is best, though they have sometimes been kept for many years.)

TURNIP SOUFFLE

2 lb turnips
1 T sugar
1 onion, sliced
3 T butter

¾ tsp salt
3 eggs, well beaten
½ tsp pepper
1 can cream of mushroom soup

Peel and cut turnips in pieces. Cook with sugar and onion until tender. Drain and mash, then mix with remaining ingredients. Place in buttered casserole dish and top with cracker crumbs and parmesan cheese. Bake 30 minutes at 350° or until firm.

BEST BEETS

1 small onion, thinly sliced
1 T plus 1 tsp butter
1 T lemon juice

1 tsp chopped parsley
1 can beets
¼ tsp salt

Saute onion lightly in butter until soft but not brown. Drain beets and place them in onion and butter. Add lemon juice and parsley. Toss beets, adding salt. Heat until hot.

(Tiny whole beets are always best.)

LITTLE NEW POTATOES IN JACKETS

Wash potatoes. Boil in salted water, cooking until a fork pierces them easily. Drain well. Add butter and chopped parsley on top of potatoes. Return to heat long enough to melt butter. Serve hot.

CORN PUDDING

2 C corn
2 T flour
1 tsp salt
3 T butter

3 whole eggs
2 T sugar
1¾ C milk

Blend butter, sugar, flour and salt. Add eggs, beating well. Stir in corn and milk. Pour ingredients in buttered casserole and bake 45 minutes at 325°. Stir once halfway through cooking. When done, the pudding will be golden brown and silver knife inserted will come out clean. We use frozen corn which we chop a little. Also delicious with fresh corn.

(The mixture can be prepared ahead of baking and kept in a jar in the refrigerator. Shake well and pour into baking dish.)

SOUTHERN GREEN BEANS

1 gal. canned green beans
½ tsp sugar
1½ T bacon grease

⅛ medium onion
1½ T ham scraps

Drain off a little more than half of the juice from the beans. Cook, adding salt and pepper to taste. They need very little if bacon grease and country ham are used. Cook slowly for about 2 hours.

(5 lbs. garden fresh green beans, to which the equivalent amount of water is added, are even better. Cook until tender, about 3 to 4 hours.)

BAKED ACORN SQUASH

1 medium acorn squash
little melted butter
¼ tsp salt

¼ tsp corn syrup (or mixture of brown and white sugar)

Scrub squash. Cut in half lengthwise; scrape out seeds and stringy portion with spoon. Brush cut surface of each half with a little melted butter. Sprinkle each half with salt, ⅛ tsp to each half. Arrange, cut side down, in a baking pan. Bake in moderate oven 400° for 30 minutes. Then turn, cut side up, and brush well with butter mixed with corn syrup. Bake until tender, about 30 minutes. Brush often with syrup butter mixture.

TRUSTEE'S SALAD

6 oz raspberry gelatin dessert
2 T chopped onion
¼ C chopped green pepper
dash tobasco

dash salt
¼ C chopped celery
1 C plus 2 T boiling water
2 C canned tomato quarters

Dissolve gelatin dessert in boiling water. Add other ingredients. Serve molded on lettuce leaf with mayonaise. Or use on Pleasant Hill Salad Plate.

KENTUCKY SALAD

2 packages lime gelatin dessert
pineapple juice and water to
   make 2 C very hot liquid
1 C cold water

2 C crushed pineapple
1½ C grated cucumber
1 tsp lemon juice

Drain pineapple and cucumber well. Make gelatin dessert according to package recipe. Cool to consistency of egg white. Fold in pineapple, cucumber and lemon juice. Pour into mold and refrigerate. Unmold and serve on crisp lettuce with mayonnaise.

(This is so cool on a hot summer day when cucumbers are in your garden.)

WINTER SALAD

6 oz lemon gelatin dessert
1½ C cold water
2 tsp salt
¼ C grated onion
2½ C small raw cauliflower

2 C boiling water
3 T vinegar
⅛ tsp pepper
¼ C diced pimiento

Dissolve gelatin in boiling water; add cold water. Toss remaining ingredients. Fold them into slightly thickened gelatin mixture.

BEAN SALAD

1 2½ can green beans	⅔ C vinegar
1 2½ can wax beans	⅓ C salad oil
1 2½ can kidney beans	½ tsp salt
¾ C sugar	½ tsp coarse pepper

Mix sugar, vinegar, oil, salt and pepper to make a dressing. Drain beans and toss them in the dressing; refrigerate, tossing frequently. If possible, let stand overnight.

GRAPEFRUIT AND AVOCADO SALAD

Peel grapefruit, removing all membrane. Cut out sections with a very sharp knife. Peel and slice avocado. Alternate sections and slices on Bibb lettuce. Serve with Honey Salad Dressing.

TOSSED SALAD

Iceberg lettuce	tomatoes
Bibb lettuce	artichoke hearts
Oakleaf lettuce	Thick French Dressing
Thin French Dressing	

Cut and toss salad greens and tomatoes. Moisten with Thin French Dressing; then fold in Thick French Dressing.

In summer top with young onions, thin unpeeled cucumber slices.

PEAR AND ROQUEFORT CHEESE SALAD

Crush and beat together ⅓ C roquefort cheese, ⅔ C cream cheese. Soften this mixture with a little cream. Fill hollow of pear with small ball of cheese mixture. Serve round side up on leaf of lettuce with a spoonful of mayonaise.

WHITE BREAD (4 ONE POUND LOAVES)

2 C milk   2 C water
¼ C sugar   1 cake yeast
4 tsp salt   ¼ C lukewarm water
8 T shortening   9 to 12 C sifted flour (approx.)

Scald milk; add sugar, salt and shortening. After shortening melts add water and cool to lukewarm. Add yeast, softened in ¼ C lukewarm water, 105° to 115°. Add flour gradually, mixing it in thoroughly. When dough is stiff, turn it onto a lightly floured board and knead until smooth and satiny. Shape into smooth ball; place in greased bowl; cover and let rise in a warm place, 80° to 85°, until almost double in bulk. Divide into four equal portions; round up each into a smooth ball. Cover well and let rest 10 to 15 minutes. Shape into loaves and place in greased loaf pans. Bake at 375° to 400° for 30 minutes or until crust sounds hollow when tapped.

(Amount of flour varies.)

CHESS PIE

½ C melted butter   1½ tsp vinegar
1½ C sugar   3 eggs
1½ tsp corn meal

Use mixer at low speed for combining ingredients, and do not mix too much. Combine sugar and melted butter; then add eggs and remaining ingredients. Pour into unbaked pie shell; use 9″ pie pans. Preheat oven to 450°. Put pie in oven and turn heat immediately to 400°. Cook at 400° about 15 minutes, then at 300° about 20 minutes. Filling for pie will puff up full. Give a little jiggle to be sure center is firm before removing it from oven. Place it on a rack to cool. Pie may be browned before serving.

(Cooking time varies as to oven and eggs; if eggs are fresh, it takes longer.)

ANGEL FOOD CAKE

1¼ C cake flour
½ C sugar
1½ C egg whites (about 12 at
    room temperature)

1¼ tsp cream of tartar
¼ tsp vanilla
1⅓ C sugar
¼ tsp salt

Measure sifted flour and add ½ C sugar. Sift this four times. Combine egg whites, cream of tartar, salt, and vanilla in large bowl. Beat at a high speed until it forms soft peaks. Sprinkle in remaining sugar in 4 additions, beating until blended well. Sift in flour 4 times. Fold in with spatula or large spoon, turning bowl often. Pour into ungreased 10 inch tube pan. Bake at 375° for 35 to 40 minutes. Cool cake upside down in pan on cake rack. Then loosen from sides and remove.

COFFEE ANGEL FOOD CAKE

Add 3 T instant coffee to dry ingredients in angel food cake recipe; this is heavenly.

FRUIT OR BERRY COBBLER

about 2 C fruit or berries
8 to 10 T sugar (depending on
    tartness of fruit)
1 T butter

2 to 3 tsp lemon juice
⅓ tsp rind
1½ T flour
dash of salt

Coat fruit with mixture of above ingredients. (Add 1 to 2 T of water if fruit seems to need juice.) Roll out one pie crust in a long, thin oval. Place fruit mixture on this; dot with butter. Roll into a long roll, like a jelly roll. Prick top with fork. Bake at 425° about 40 minutes. Slice and serve warm.

PRUNE CAKE

2 C flour
½ tsp salt
1 tsp soda
1 tsp cinnamon
1½ C sugar
3 eggs

1 C salad oil
1 tsp vanilla
1 C buttermilk
1 C cooked prunes
1 C nuts

Sift together flour, salt, soda and cinnamon. Set aside. Mix thoroughly sugar, eggs, oil, vanilla, and buttermilk. Add flour mixture. Fold in cooked chopped prunes and nuts. Bake 45 minutes to 1 hour at 325° in greased baking pan. Serve with Prune Cake Sauce. (See below.)

PRUNE CAKE SAUCE

½ C melted butter
1 C sugar
½ C buttermilk

¼ tsp soda
¼ tsp vanilla

Make this sauce 10 minutes before prune cake is done. Boil all ingredients together for two minutes, stirring constantly. When cake is done, prick it immediately with fork and pour the sauce over it while it is hot.

WHOLE PECAN COOKIES

1 unbeaten egg white
¾ C light brown sugar

1 tsp vanilla
2 C nuts

Stir egg white, light brown sugar and vanilla together. Stir in pecans until they are coated with the mixture.

Grease and flour a cookie sheet. Lift up three pecans with two forks and place them on a cookie sheet. Repeat until all pecans are used. (If mixture is left, add more pecans.)

Preheat the oven at 350° for 10 minutes. Place in oven. Turn oven off immediately and leave cookies for 50 minutes. Store in tins.

PEANUT BUTTER COOKIES

½ C butter

½ C firmly packed brown sugar

½ C granulated sugar

½ C peanut butter

1 egg

½ tsp vanilla

½ tsp salt

½ tsp soda

1 C flour

Cream butter and peanuts butter until well blended. Add both kinds of sugar. Beat egg slightly and add to sugar and butter mixture. Sift dry ingredients together and add to creamy mixture; add more flour if dough is not quite stiff enough. Add vanilla. Drop by tsp onto greased cookie sheet. Press gently with sugared fork; this step is important to the flavor of the cookies, as they cook more quickly and get a better consistency. Bake at 350° until light brown—about 10 minutes.

SPICY GINGERBREAD

2½ C flour

1½ tsp baking soda

¼ tsp ground cloves

1 tsp cinnamon

1 tsp ginger

¾ tsp salt

½ C shortening

½ C sugar

1 unbeaten egg

1 C molasses (dark)

1 C hot water

Line baking pan with waxed paper. Sift flour, soda, salt and spices. In large mixing bowl cream shortening and sugar; then add egg. Beat until light and fluffy. Beat in molasses. Alternately and slowly beat in flour mixture and hot water. (Raisins may be added to batter.)

Turn into greased pan. Bake at 350° about 35 minutes or until firm in center.

(The old fashioned way to test for doneness is to insert a clean broom straw and test to see that nothing sticks.)

Notes

Shakertown at Pleasant Hill
Trustees' House
Sunday and Holiday Daily Fare

Soup of Day   Fruit Juice
Tomato Juice   Egg in Aspic

Relishes ~ ~ Corn Sticks

Fried Chicken
Country Ham
Combination Fried Chicken and Country Ham

Vegetables and Salad will be passed

Village Hot Breads

Shaker Lemon Pie   Chess Pie
Seasonal Tart
Ice Cream or Ice

Coffee   Milk   Tea   Buttermilk

GUMBO SOUP

1 2½ can tomatoes
1 tsp chopped parsley
½ gallon chicken broth
   (Bouillon cubes may be used
   to make broth.)
1 C lima beans
½ chopped green pepper
1 bay leaf
½ tiny red pepper (or ground
   red pepper to taste)

1 pt okra (box frozen)
¼ tsp black pepper
½ C cubed or chopped ham
   (We use country ham.)
1 C chopped onion
1 tsp salt (or to taste)
1 T flour
filé powder to taste
   (optional)

Combine all ingredients except flour and seasoning; simmer one hour. Add seasoning and thicken with flour mixed with water to make a thin paste.

TOMATO CELERY SOUP

1 small chopped onion
2 T butter
1 10½ oz can tomato soup
1 tsp minced parsley
⅛ tsp pepper

½ C finely chopped celery
1 T lemon juice
1 tsp sugar
¼ tsp salt
1 can water

Saute onion and celery in butter; do not brown. Add tomato soup, water, parsley, lemon juice, sugar, salt and pepper. Simmer 5 minutes. Celery will remain crisp.

Top with unsweetened whipped cream and chopped parsley.

SPICED HOT TOMATO JUICE

1 large can tomato juice
2 tsp Worcestershire sauce
1 tsp seasoning salt

1¾ tsp salt
1¾ tsp tobasco

Heat, but do not boil, juice combined with other ingredients. Serve in small glasses topped with unsweetened whipped cream sprinkled with parsley.

RELISH BOWL

Place celery hearts in a very large wooden bowl. Fill in the sides with olives, both stuffed green and ripe. Add pickled okra and tiny pickled ears of corn; add sweet and dill pickle slices. Fresh salad vegetables may be added when they are in season. Especially good are cauliflower flowerettes, sliced cucumbers, spring onions, radishes, and cherry tomatoes.

CUCUMBER PICKLE

5½ lbs ripe yellow cucumbers	1 qt vinegar
little tumeric	3½ to 4 C sugar
1 T whole cloves	3 or 4 cinnamon sticks
mustard seed	

Peel, seed and cut up cucumbers. Put in one gallon of lime water and let stand overnight. Drain. Wash through two or three waters. Put in kettle with vinegar and sugar and allow to come to a boil. for a few minutes; then add cloves, mustard seed, cinnamon sticks; add tumeric for color. Let boil until pickles take yellow color; then strain off syrup. Pack sterilized jars with pickles. Boil syrup until it thickens a little; pour it over the pickles and seal.

SWEET PICKLES AND ONIONS

6 qts sliced cucumbers	½ C mustard seed
5 C sugar	1 tsp. tumeric
1 T celery seed	salt water
6 sliced onions	1¼ qts. cider vinegar

Slice onions and cucumbers. Cover with salt water and allow to stand for 3 hours. Drain. Place sugar, mustard seed, celery seed, and tumeric in vinegar. Bring spices and vinegar to a boil. Place in sterilized jars and seal.

CORN STICKS

½ tsp salt
½ tsp soda
3 tsp sugar
½ tsp baking powder
2 T oil

1 egg
½ C flour
1 C buttermilk
1 C plus 2 T corn meal

Beat all ingredients together, beating well. Heat greased irons until hot enough to sizzle. Fill irons to half full. Bake at 450° about 10 minutes or until brown.

(The secret of good corn bread is beating well and using hot irons.)

FRIED CHICKEN

1 frying chicken
1 C flour

salt and pepper to taste

Dip chicken pieces in flour mixed with salt and pepper. The simplest and best way to cover chicken with flour is to shake them together in a paper bag.

Heat about ½ inch shortening in a heavy skillet. Place flour covered chicken, meaty side down, in skillet. When golden brown, turn and fry until well done and tender. Keep heat low; do not hurry the frying. Let excess grease drip off on paper towel before serving.

TURKEY IN FOIL

Put the stuffed and trussed turkey in the center of a large piece of aluminum foil. Brush the turkey with melted butter or margarine; bring foil up over the bird and seal all edges together. Seal does not have to be perfect. Place on rack in open roasting pan; roast in preheated oven according to the following chart:

COOKING TIME

Stuffed Weight In Lbs	Cooking Time Minutes Per Lb.	Hours Per Bird
8 to 10 lbs	18	2½ to 3
11 to 14	17	3 to 3¾
15 to 18	15	3¾ to 4½
19 to 24	14	4½ to 5½

Cook at 400°; turkey is done when leg pulls away easily. During the last 45 minutes of roasting time open and fold back foil. The juice is a small amount, but it is concentrated and will make a good gravy. (Basting is unnecessary; spoon a little melted shortening over the bird when foil is removed.) Simmer giblets, neck and liver in water and use for gravy.

DRESSING BALLS

¾ stick butter
2 tsp chopped parsley
1 lb stale bread crumbs (6½ C)
1 beaten egg
black pepper
poultry seasoning

2½ T chopped celery
1 small chopped onion
chicken broth
salt
seasoning salt

Saute celery, parsley and onion in butter. Add bread crumbs. Add chicken broth until consistency is right for molding. Stir in egg and add seasonings to taste. Mold into 2″ balls. Bake at 350° for about 20 minutes. Serve immediately. Makes 10 balls.

(Some corn bread in the bread crumbs is good.)

SCALLOPED OYSTERS

1 pt oysters
6 T cream and oyster liquor
1½ C coarse cracker crumbs

salt and pepper
½ C melted butter

Pick over oysters and drain. Grease the baking dish and cover the bottom with a third of the crumbs. Cover with half of the oysters and season. Add half of the oyster liquor and cream. Repeat. Cover the top with remaining crumbs. Pour melted butter over all. Bake at 400° for about 30 minutes.

(This makes your Thanksgiving or Christmas a success.)

CRANBERRY SAUCE

2 C sugar
4 C cranberries

2 C water

Boil sugar and water together 5 minutes. Add cranberries and boil without stirring until all skins pop—about 5 to 10 minutes to desired thickness; we like it well jelled. Remove from fire; allow sauce to remain in pan until cooled.

PLEASANT HILL BAKED EGGPLANT

1 large eggplant
½ medium onion
2 T butter
3 T chopped parsley

dash of Worcestershire sauce
salt and pepper to taste
butter crackers (not Saltine)
1 can cream of mushroom soup

Cut top off eggplant lengthwise. Scrape out the inside, leaving about ½ inch around sides and bottom of shell. Boil eggplant meat in salted water until it is tender. Drain completely and chop. Saute chopped onion in butter and add chopped parsley. Mix with eggplant and soup; add seasonings. Mix with enough crumbled crackers to make a good stuffing consistency. Pile filling back into eggplant shell. Sprinkle with cracker crumbs and dot with butter. Bake at 375° for 30 to 35 minutes.

SPICED APPLES

1 C water   1 C sugar
6 apples   ¼ C cinnamon drops

Boil water, sugar and cinnamon drops until cinnamon drops are dissolved. Peel and core apples. Slice in rings. Add them to syrup and cook until tender. Remove apples; set them aside. Boil syrup until thick. Pour it over apples. Serve warm.

CUSHAW

Peel a ripe cushaw and cut it into good-sized pieces. Sprinkle it with a mixture of brown and granulated sugar. Dot it with butter and bake in a buttered baking dish at 375° until tender.

(If your family likes squash, consider this economical variety too often by-passed. If your family dislikes squash, introduce it as "cushaw.")

BLACKEYED PEAS

Boil the peas, fresh or frozen, for about 30 minutes. Season them with salt, pepper and butter. Country ham fat may be used in place of butter.

(Eat these on New Year's Day to bring the Best of Luck in the new year.)

SQUASH CASSEROLE

2 lbs squash (yellow or zucchini)   ¾ tsp salt
3 T butter   ½ tsp pepper
3 eggs beaten   1 onion sliced
1 can cream of mushroom soup

Cook squash and onion until tender. Drain and mash. Fold in remaining ingredients. Place in buttered casserole dish and top with cracker crumbs and Parmesan cheese. Bake at 350° for 30 minutes.

BING CHERRY SALAD

2 packages cherry gelatin dessert
1 2½ can sweet bing cherries (or
    pitted dark red cherries)
juice from cherries

1 C port or sherry wine
2 T lemon juice
2 C boiling water

Pour boiling water over gelatin dessert and stir well. Add 1 C cherry juice, wine and lemon juice. When mixture is cool, fold in cherries and mold.

AUTUMN SALAD

1 package lemon gelatin dessert
1 C crushed pineapple
1 T vinegar

1 C shredded carrots
2 C boiling water
few grains salt

Dissolve gelatin in boiling water. Cool until partially set. Add vegetables, pineapple, vinegar and salt. Pour into mold. Chill until firm. Serve on crisp lettuce with mayonaise.

MOLDED CRANBERRY SALAD

1 package rasberry gelatin dessert
½ C pineapple juice and ½ C
    water
1 package cranberries

½ C cold water
2 C sugar
2 oranges (quartered and
    seeded)

Boil mixture of pineapple juice and water; add to gelatin dessert and stir well until gelatin is dissolved. Add cold water. Put cranberries through food chopper. Add sugar and mix well. When gelatin cools to consistency of egg white, fold in chopped cranberries and orange quarters. Pour into mold and chill until firm.

CRUST FOR ONE PIE

1 C flour	⅓ C plus 2 T shortening
½ tsp salt	2 T cold water

Mix flour and salt. Cut shortening into flour until it forms very small balls. Sprinkle in water, a T at a time, while mixing lightly with a fork until the flour is moistened. Mix it into a ball that cleans the bowl. Do not overwork the dough. Roll out on floured board and place in pie pan.

(The less you handle dough, the better; handling toughens it. A good crust must be crisp, even at the risk of being a bit crumbly. Sometimes a tougher pie crust looks more perfect, but this is one case where you must choose between appearance and taste.)

PUMPKIN PIE

1 C pumpkin	3 eggs
⅔ C sugar (maple or brown)	2 C milk
½ tsp ginger	1 unbaked pie shell
½ tsp cinnamon	½ tsp salt

Mix all ingredients together. Blend thoroughly. Pour into unbaked pie shell and bake in moderate oven, 350°, until silver knife inserted comes out clean.

TART SHELLS FOR 12 TARTS

1 C flour	⅓ C shortening plus 1 T
½ tsp salt	2 T water

Mix flour and salt. Cut shortening into flour until it forms very small balls. Sprinkle in water a little at a time while mixing lightly with a fork until flour is moistened; mix into a ball that cleans the bowl. Do not overwork. Roll out on a floured board. Cut in circles to cover small tart molds. Pierce with a fork and trim. Cover with extra mold and bake 6 to 8 minutes at 475°. Remove top mold and brown slightly. Browning takes about 2 minutes.

(Tarts may be filled with fruits in season: fresh peaches, strawberries, black or red raspberries.)

MINCEMEAT TART

Season mincemeat with bourbon to taste. Spoon into prepared tart shell. Serve with unsweetened whipped cream. Top with a turkey pastry made by cutting a small turkey with cookie cutter from pie crust recipe.

(This recipe is a very simple dessert for those holiday meals.)

COCONUT CREAM TARTS

¼ C granulated sugar
¼ C plus 1 T flour
¼ tsp salt
2 C milk
shredded coconut

2 egg yolks beaten
  with ¼ C sugar
¼ C sugar
1 T butter
1 tsp vanilla

Combine sugar, flour and salt in a double boiler; stir in milk slowly. Cook over boiling water until thick as custard sauce. Cover and cook 12 minutes longer, stirring occasionally. Stir a little of this hot mixture into egg yolks that have been beaten with sugar; then stir into mixture in double boiler. Cook about 2 minutes or until thick. Remove from heat and add butter and vanilla. Cool. Pour into baked tart shell. Top with unsweetened whipped cream. Sprinkle generously with coconut.

CARAMEL TARTS

2 C light brown sugar
4 egg yolks
¼ C plus 2 T flour

4 tsp butter
2 C cold water
1½ tsp vanilla

Beat egg yolks slightly. Add brown sugar mixed with flour. Put in double boiler and gradually stir in water. Cook until thick, then add butter and vanilla. Serve in tart shells topped with unsweetened whipped cream sprinkled with brown sugar.

CHOCOLATE TARTS

¼ C sugar
¼ C plus 2 T flour
¼ tsp salt
2 C milk

2 egg yolks beaten
with ¼ C sugar
1 T butter
2 squares chocolate

In top of double boiler mix sugar, flour and salt. Place over heat and gradually add milk and chopped chocolate squares. Cook, stirring occasionally, until thick. Cover and cook 12 minutes longer. This may need more stirring. Stir a little of this hot mixture into egg yolks beaten with sugar; then combine this with the mixture in the double boiler. Cook 2 minutes longer and remove from stove. Cool and serve in baked tart shells. Top with unsweetened whipped cream.

(Stirring a small amount of hot mixture into eggs and sugar keeps the eggs from cooking too quickly.)

CANDIED GRAPEFRUIT PEEL

3 grapefruit
2 T corn syrup

1 qt cold water
1 T salt

Wipe grapefruit and remove peel in 4 sections lengthwise of fruit. Soak overnight in cold water in which salt has been dissolved. Drain; cover with cold water; bring to boiling point and boil 20 minutes. Repeat this process 3 times and cook in the last water until soft—about 4 hours. Drain and cut in strips ⅛ inch wide. Weigh peel; put an equal weight of sugar in saucepan and half as much water. Add corn syrup. Bring to a boil; add peel; cover and cook until peel is clear and almost dry (to 230°). Remove to place, taking up as little syrup as possible. Cool. Roll each piece in granulated sugar; spread on waxed paper to dry. Store in glass jars.

HOLIDAY COOKIE BALLS

1 C butter   ½ C powdered sugar
½ C chopped pecans   1¾ C flour
¼ tsp salt   ½ tsp vanilla

Cream the butter well. Gradually add sugar; cream thoroughly. Add salt, vanilla, flour and nuts; mix well. Chill 1 hour for easy handling. Form into small balls. Bake at 350° for 20 minutes on ungreased cookie sheet. Immediately after balls are removed from oven, roll them in powdered sugar; let cool on rack.

PARFAIT

To assemble a parfait put about one inch of vanilla ice cream in a parfait glass (a tall, footed glass); add about one tablespoon desired sauce. Alternate layers to fill glass. Top with whipped cream, and add mint leaf or any suitable decoration.

(Bourbon, Chocolate, Mint, Maple or any sauce you like may be used. These can be kept frozen; add whipped cream and decoration at the last minute for a very attractive and easy dessert.)

CHRISTMAS SNOW CREAM

2 qts newly fallen snow   vanilla
cream   granulated sugar

You must make this very quickly and eat it immediately. Mix cream and vanilla together. (Snow cream should be flavored to taste; that is why no proportions are given.) After collecting snow, take a large chilled bowl and put snow in layers, sprinkling sugar on each layer. Fold flavored cream into snow, being sure not to let the cream fall to the bottom of the bowl. Toss snow constantly; it will freeze the cream.

(When the Trustees' House was snowed in, Christmas 1969, we made this and served it to guests Christmas night; it makes a light and delicious dessert.)

Notes

Special Daily Fare

SPICED TEA

4 qts boiling water	16 whole cloves
2 C sugar	16 allspice
3 tea bags	1 stick cinnamon
juice of 2 oranges	juice of 4 lemons

Put allspice and cloves in cheesecloth bag. Place water, spice bag and sugar in pan; boil ten minutes. Remove spice bag. Add tea bags and brew 3 to 5 minutes; put cinnamon stick in while brewing. Remove tea bags and cinnamon stick. Add juice. Heat carefully before serving; do not boil.

SHAKER SPICED APPLE CIDER

3 qts cider	1 whole clove
1 stick cinnamon	½ C sugar
1 whole nutmeg	

Place spices in cheesecloth bag. Put cider, sugar and bag in pan and simmer for at least 3 minutes. Serve hot in warmed cups.

SOUP FOR A HOT SUMMER DAY

1 medium onion	juice of 2 limes
1 cucumber	1½ T wine vinegar
1 green pepper	1½ tsp Worestershire sauce
fresh tomato	1 drop tobasco sauce
radishes	1 clove garlic
celery	¼ tsp dry mustard
1 qt tomato juice	2 tsp olive oil
freshly ground pepper	2 hard boiled eggs
1 tsp salt	

Grind onion, cucumber, seeded pepper, tomatoes, radishes and celery. Mix tomato juice, lime juice, vinegar, Worcestershire sauce, tobasco sauce, garlic, salt, pepper and mashed or ground eggs. Make a paste of mustard and olive oil. Add this to the soup and mix well. Chill at least 2 hours. Serve very cold topped with an ice cube and a thin slice of lime.

(Anything and everything can go into this soup—even cold shrimp. Use your imagination.)

PEASE PORRIDGE SOUP

Saute 1 small chopped onion in 1 T bacon grease or butter. Add a country ham bone, 1 stalk celery, 1¾ cup split peas and 6½ C cold water. Season with salt, seasoning salt and pepper to taste. Simmer until peas are well done (about 50 minutes.) Press through sieve. Add ham from bone to soup and serve with croutons.

THIN WHITE SAUCE

1 T butter	¼ tsp salt
1 T flour	⅛ tsp pepper
1 C milk	

MEDIUM WHITE SAUCE

2 T butter	¼ tsp salt
2 T flour	⅛ tsp pepper
1 C milk	

THICK WHITE SAUCE

¼ C butter	¼ tsp salt
¼ C flour	⅛ tsp pepper
1 C milk	

Melt butter in a saucepan. Using a wire wisk or a wooden spoon, blend in flour, salt and pepper. Cook, stirring constantly, until smooth—about 1 minute. Remove from heat and stir in milk. Bring to a boil; it is important to stir while mixture is coming to a boil. Boil 1 minute.

MUSHROOM CREAM SAUCE

3 T butter
¼ C flour
1½ C warm milk
1½ C canned unsweetened
  condensed milk

sliced mushroom buttons (if
  fresh, brown lightly in butter)
dash paprika
salt and pepper to taste

Melt butter in top of double boiler; then add flour, pepper, salt and paprika, while stirring with a wire wisk until blended and smooth. Add milk slowly, stirring constantly to prevent lumps. Cook until smooth and thickened, stirring constantly. Add mushrooms. Serve with Cream de Volaille and Chicken Croquettes.

TARTAR SAUCE

1 pt mayonaise
2 T chopped onions
dash of salt and black pepper

1 chopped dill pickle
⅛ tsp red pepper
1 T capers (optional)

Mix all together. Serve with fried fish.

CHEESE WAFERS

1 C butter
2 C flour
½ lb sharp cheese

1 beaten egg
pecans

Mix butter, flour and cheese all together with your hands; then roll out on floured board and cut with a very small buiscuit cutter. Place on cookie sheet and brush tops with beaten egg. Put pecan on top of each and bake at 350° for 10 minutes. As soon as you take them out of the oven, sprinkle them with salt and remove them from the cookie sheet. Makes about 75 wafers.

(These are delicious as snacks and tid-bits. You may leave the pecans off some of them for variety; they are just as good.)

CHEESE LOAF

1½ lb cheese
1 small can stuffed olives, drained
½ C or more pecans
1 C whipping cream
¾ pt country dressing

1 small can pimientos, drained
2 T plain gelatin
½ tsp salt
⅛ tsp red pepper
¼ tsp tobasco sauce

Grate or grind cheese. Finely chop olives, pimientos and nuts. Soak gelatin in cold water according to directions on package and dissolve by setting cup in boiling water. Add country dressing to cheese; add olives, pecans, pimientos, nuts, salt, pepper and tobasco. Add gelatin. Whip cream and fold it in last. Place in mold that has been rinsed with cold water. Refrigerate until firm. Turn out and decorate with whole pecans and sliced stuffed olives.

CHEESE BALLS

1½ C flour
½ lb sharp grated cheese
½ C melted butter

10 to 12 drops tobasco sauce
dash garlic salt
10 oz jar stuffed olives, drained

Combine flour, cheese, butter, tobasco sauce and garlic salt. Wrap around olives, making a small ball. Freeze until ready to bake. Bake on ungreased cookie sheet at 375° for 15 to 20 minutes. Makes about 50 balls.

PIMIENTO CHEESE

3 inch block American cheese
2 whole pimientos

1½ inch block cheddar cheese
mayonnaise

Grind or grate ingredients together. Add mayonnaise to desired consistency.

CHIVES DIP

3 8 oz packages cream cheese   ¼ tsp garlic salt
6 T half and half   dash of salt
3 T mayonnaise   1 T grated onion
1 tsp celery salt   3 to 4 T chopped chives

Cream the cream cheese. Add other ingredients and mix well. Serve at room temperature with potato chips or crackers.

(For variety serve chilled raw carrot and celery strips, which are delicious with this dip. A few ice cubes on the relishes will keep them fresh in your refrigerator until ready to serve.)

CRAB OR SHRIMP DIP

1 C mayonnaise   1 6½ oz can crabmeat or
1 T chopped parsley   shrimp (or lobster)
1 T sherry   1 tsp lemon juice
½ C sour cream

Combine all ingredients, mixing well; chill 2 hours before serving. You may want to add more lemon juice, but be careful; this dip is rather runny in consistency.

GERMAN POTATO SALAD

7 medium potatoes	¾ C water
1 small onion	3 to 4 tsp sugar
3 strips of bacon	2 tsp corn starch
(cooked, but still limp, not crisp)	¾ C vinegar

Cook potatoes and chill; then slice. Cook bacon; remove and chop. In skillet after cooking bacon saute onion until soft (not brown.) Stir in corn starch, sugar, water and vinegar. Place potatoes and bacon in mixture; toss gently. Cover and let heat a moment. Remove.

(If you are a good German cook, you will have the potatoes cold and the bacon limp. Let the salad stand before serving; the longer it stands, the better the flavor.)

LEMON-LIME SUMMER SALAD

1 package lemon gelatin dessert	1 No. 2 can crushed pineapple
1 package lime gelatin dessert	1 small can evaporated milk
1 C mayonnaise	2 C boiling water
1 C chopped pecans	1 lb small curd cottage cheese

Combine lime and lemon gelatin with each other, then with the mayonnaise, mixing well. Add boiling water and continue mixing until dissolved. Add milk. Pour into mold and add pineapple and cottage cheese to mold. Be sure to mix gently as you add. Add nuts the same way. Gently stir to distribute evenly around the mold. Unmold on lettuce and serve with mayonnaise.

You may make this in layers: chill a little mixture in the mold before adding pineapple and cottage cheese. Fold cottage cheese and pineapple into remaining mixture and place in mold when first layer is firm. Then press pecans in last, pressing into gelatin as a thin 'crust' on the bottom.

HONEY SALAD DRESSING

⅔ C sugar
1 tsp paprika
¼ tsp salt
5 T vinegar
1 T onion juice

1 tsp dry mustard
1 tsp celery seed
⅓ C strained honey
1 T lemon juice
1 C salad oil

Mix thoroughly with electric mixer, adding salad oil last.

THIN FRENCH DRESSING

6 T oil
2 T vinegar
¼ tsp salt
sliver of onion

a little lemon juice
1 tsp sugar
¼ tsp paprika

Put all ingredients in dressing bottle. Shake well before use.

THICK FRENCH DRESSING

2 eggs
6 T sugar
¾ C vinegar
½ tsp salt
2 C salad oil

1 tsp paprika
¾ tsp Worcestershire sauce
¾ tsp seasoning salt
¼ tsp coarse black pepper
¼ tsp red pepper

Mix very well. This is best if made in blender.

GINGER SALAD DRESSING

⅓ C mayonnaise
2 T chopped candied ginger

⅓ C whipped cream

Mix mayonnaise and whipped cream. Fold in ginger. Serve with
October Salad .

BLUE CHEESE DRESSING

½ C salad oil
2 T lemon juice
½ tsp dry mustard
¼ tsp paprika
¼ C crumbled blue cheese

2 T vinegar
1 tsp salt
1 tsp sugar
½ tsp Worcestershire sauce

Blend well. Refrigerate and mix well before tossing salad.

COUNTRY DRESSING

1 tsp dry mustard
2 T sugar
¼ tsp salt
2 T flour

½ C cold water
2 egg yolks
¼ C vinegar
2 T butter

Dissolve mustard, sugar, salt and flour in water. Beat eggs and vinegar in top of double boiler. Add the dissolved ingredients. Cook and stir the dressing over boiling water until thick and smooth. Add butter. Use for chicken salad, cole slaw and country ham salad.

(Egg whites may be frozen and saved until you have enough to make a delicious Angel Food Cake.)

SHAKER WHEATEN BREAD

1 C milk
1 T salt
3 T butter
4 T honey or maple syrup

1 cake yeast
1 C warm water
2 C sifted flour
4 C whole wheat flour

Scald milk; add salt, butter, syrup and ¾ C of warm water; stir well. Let cool to lukewarm. In the remaining ¼ C water dissolve the yeast; add to other mixture. Add flours gradually and knead into a smooth ball. Place in buttered bowl and brush top with soft butter. Let rise to double its bulk. Knead lightly this time and shape into loaf in pan. Again brush with soft butter and let rise to twice its bulk. Bake at 350° for 50 to 60 minutes.

SPOON BREAD

1 C corn meal
1 qt sweet milk
3 eggs

1¾ tsp salt
½ tsp baking powder
2 T butter

Scald milk and add meal gradually. Cook until thick. Pour small amount over beaten egg yolks; then add egg yolks. Return to heat and cook a few minutes longer. Add butter and fold in beaten egg whites; add baking powder and salt. Pour into greased baking dish and cook at 325° for 1½ hours. Stir once after first 15 minutes of cooking.

HUSH PUPPIES

2 C corn meal
1 tsp salt
⅔ C milk

2 tsp baking powder
finely chopped onion (optional)
1 egg

Mix corn meal, baking powder and salt; add onion if desired. Stir in milk and egg. Mold in round balls about the size of golf balls and fry in hot fish fat.

CARAWAY HORNS

3 tsp shortening
3 tsp sugar
½ cake yeast
2 T lukewarm water
caraway seeds

1 egg
¾ tsp salt
½ C milk
3 C flour

Cream shortening and sugar. Add beaten egg. Dissolve yeast in water and add to mixture. Add flour to make a stiff dough. Knead smooth. Cover and let rise until double in bulk. Divide into two portions. Roll out into circle; cut in 8 wedge-shaped pieces. Roll up each piece, starting at the wide end; shape into half circles. Brush with melted butter; sprinkle with caraway seeds and coarse salt. Place on a baking sheet and cover with a clean cloth towel. Let stand 1 hour or until double in bulk. Remove towel and bake at 425° for 10 minutes.

HOLLANDAISE SAUCE

1 stick butter
½ tsp red pepper (to taste)
about 1 C boiling water
¼ C lemon juice

½ C flour
1 tsp salt
4 lightly beaten egg yolks

Mix flour into melted butter in a small double boiler. Add salt and red pepper. Add boiling water; stirring constantly, add egg yolks, then lemon juice and continue stirring. An electric mixer is best. Serve hot.

HARD SAUCE

½ C butter
pinch of salt

1 C granulated sugar
(or brown)
1 tsp vanilla (or 2 T brandy)

Cream butter with sugar, beating until very light. Add salt, then flavoring. Put into refrigerator until firm.

VANILLA SAUCE FOR SPICE PUDDINGS

1 tsp vanilla
½ C sugar
1 T corn starch
1 C boiling water

2 T butter
few grains nutmeg
few grains salt

Mix sugar and corn starch. Gradually add the boiling water. Boil 5 minutes. Remove from heat and add other ingredients. Serve hot.

MINT SAUCE

1 C sugar
½ C water

2 T corn syrup
essence of peppermint
green food coloring

Mix sugar, water and corn syrup in saucepan. Cook 20 minutes. Add peppermint to taste, but be careful; essence of peppermint goes a long way. Add coloring. Cover and store in refrigerator.

(Mint parfait may be made ahead of time and stored in the freezer. Serve it topped with unsweetened whipped cream and a sprig of mint.)

BOURBON SAUCE FOR ICE CREAM

1 C brown sugar
1 scant cup water

1 C white sugar

Mix and boil until it spins a thread. Then add:

1 C strawberry preserves
juice of one lemon
grated lemon rind
1 C nuts (pecans or English
    walnuts, or a mixture of both.)

1 orange in small sections
grated orange rind
½ C whiskey

Put it in the refrigerator and let it ripen. It gets better as time goes on.

HOT FUDGE PECAN BALLS

Dip ice cream and form into balls. Roll in chopped nuts and freeze. Serve with hot fudge sauce. (See below.)

HOT FUDGE SAUCE

6 squares bitter chocolate   1 C cream
1⅔ C sugar   ⅓ C butter
dash of salt

Melt chocolate and butter in heavy saucepan; add cream and blend. Add sugar and cook to desired thickness, about 7 minutes. Beat until smooth.

PRALINE CHIP

1½ C granulated sugar   ¾ C nuts

Melt sugar slowly; when melted add the nuts and let cook until caramel color. Pour on marble slab and let cool until cold. When cold pound to a powder and put in a sealed jar. This is for use in maple parfait or in sundaes.

MAPLE PARFAIT

¾ C maple syrup   6 egg yolks
½ C praline chip (See above.)   1 qt whipped cream

Cook syrup and egg yolks in a double boiler, stirring constantly. Cook until thick enough to coat a spoon. Pour into a bowl and beat until cold. Whip cream separately; them fold it slowly into the maple mixture. Add praline dust. Place in mold and freeze.

(When I was a child, this was put in heavy molds and buried in the snow on cold, snowy days.)

FRUIT ICE

3 pt water   3 C sugar
3 lemons   3 bananas
3 oranges

Make a simple syrup of sugar and water by boiling together for 3 minutes. Squeeze juice of lemons and oranges; add to syrup. Mash banana and fold it in; freeze. When lightly frozen, take out and beat with a mixer quickly in a cold bowl. Finish freezing.

SIMPLE SHAKER COOKIES

½ C butter   1½ C flour
¾ C granulated sugar   1 tsp baking powder
1 egg   ¼ tsp salt
1 tsp vanilla

Cream butter and sugar until well blended. Beat in egg and vanilla, mixing well. Sift dry ingredients together. Add this to creamed mixture. Chill for at least two hours, then roll and cut on floured surface. (This dough can be rolled in a wax paper cylinder and sliced and baked after chilling. For cookie presses omit the chilling.) Place on a greased cookie sheet. Bake at 400° until firm but not brown.

(This recipe has many uses. It's basic for fancy-shaped holiday cookies, plain icebox cookies or drop cookies.)

MULBERRY COBBLER

4 T lemon juice   1 C self rising flour
1 qt mulberries   1 C sugar
1⅓ C sugar   1 C milk
½ C butter

Sweeten mulberries with 1⅓ C sugar; add lemon juice. Cook until quite hot. Melt butter in pan; add mulberries to it. Mix flour, sugar and milk; pour mixture through a strainer into mulberries. Bake at 450° about 50 minutes or until brown. No top crust is necessary, since the dough cooks up between the berries.

(The Shakers raised silkworms and made silk. Their mulberry trees no longer have silk worms, but they produce excellent cobblers.)

WOODFORD PUDDING

½ C butter   1 C sugar
1 C flour   1 C blackberry jam
1 tsp soda   ½ C sour milk
1 full tsp cinnamon   3 eggs

Mix all together well. Bake in pudding dish at 375° for 40 minutes or until lightly firm.

SUGAR PIE

3 eggs   ¼ tsp salt
2 C brown sugar   ¼ stick butter

Cream butter and sugar. Beat eggs separately and add; mix well. Put in uncooked pie shell. Bake at 300° or 325° for 40 minutes or until firm.

(This is an adventure: it never cooks the same way twice!)

MERINGUE FOR ONE PIE

3 egg whites   dash of salt
6 T granulated sugar

Add salt to egg whites. Beat until peaks form; then add sugar, 1 T at a time, beating after each addition. Continue beating until stiff and glossy, but not dry. Bake at 375° until light brown, about 10 to 12 minutes.

COUNTRY THUMB COOKIES

½ C butter
¼ C light brown sugar, packed
1 egg yolk
⅓ C finely chopped pecans,
  walnuts or filberts

½ tsp vanilla
1 C flour
¼ tsp salt
jelly or preserves

Cream butter, sugar, salt, egg yolk and vanilla. Gradually stir in flour, blending well. Cover and chill until firm enough to handle. Work with half of the dough at a time, keeping the remainder in the refrigerator. Shape dough into nickel-sized balls; roll balls in chopped nuts. Place them 1 inch apart on ungreased cookie sheet. Gently press thumb into center of cookie. Then fill the indentation with jelly. Bake in preheated oven at 350° until light brown, about 15 minutes. Store in refrigerator in tins. Makes 3 dozen cookies.

(This cookie can be baked with indentation and later filled with a drop of thick glaze.)

PECAN CLUSTER COOKIES

1 egg white
¾ C light brown sugar

1 tsp vanilla
2 C pecans

Beat egg white and sugar until mixture is light and sugar is dissolved. Add vanilla. Toss the nuts in this until they are coated. Drop by spoonful onto greased and floured cookie sheet, dropping about three pecans to each cookie.

Preheat oven to 350° for 10 minutes. Put cookie sheet in oven and turn off heat. Let cookies sit in oven for 50 minutes. Store in tins.

WEDDING OR PARTY PUNCH

3 large bottles ginger ale
1 16 oz can frozen lemonade
46 oz water

1 large bottle soda water
1 package frozen sliced
  strawberries

Place block of ice in center of punch bowl. Pour chilled ingredients over ice. Makes 1 bowl of punch, about 25 cups.

Index

74